The OTHER SIDE of the SAME COIN

ANG SOO KEE

ISBN 978-981-94-7278-9

This book is intended for educational and informational purposes only. The views expressed are those of the author and should not be construed as investment, legal or financial advice. Readers should seek professional advice before making any investment or business decisions.

The examples and case studies in this book are intended to illustrate investor relations concepts. References to companies are based on publicly available information and are used solely for educational purposes.

First published in 2026

Published by Ang Soo Kee

CONTENTS

Preface

Investor Relations (IR) is one of the most misunderstood professions in the capital markets. To some, it is an administrative function responsible for organising meetings, preparing presentation slides, arranging roadshows and serving as the communication channel between investors and management. To others, it is simply a public relations role focused on creating a positive image for the company and supporting its share price. Both views are incomplete. At its best, IR is neither administration nor marketing. It is a strategic function that helps the capital market understand the true value of a company.

Every listed company competes for capital. Investors have thousands of companies to choose from and cannot study every business in detail. Instead, they rely on information, analysis and communication to decide where to invest. A company with an excellent business but poor communication may remain undervalued because the market does not fully appreciate its strengths. Conversely, a company with an attractive story but weak fundamentals may attract temporary attention, but sooner or later the market will recognise the difference between promise and performance. Over the long term, sustainable shareholder value is created when strong business performance is matched by market understanding and investor confidence. This is where IR makes a meaningful contribution.

In my view, the role of IR is to help the market recognise a company's underlying value by building trust and improving understanding. This is achieved by ***communicating*** *the company's strategy, business model and long-term outlook clearly;* ***managing expectations*** *by ensuring that investors have a realistic understanding of what management intends to achieve; and* ***building trust*** *by keeping market expectations aligned with management's delivery over time.*

Trust becomes particularly important during difficult periods. Good news is easy to communicate, but the true test of IR comes when business conditions deteriorate, earnings disappoint or unexpected events occur. During such periods, credibility becomes more important than optimism. Companies that communicate honestly and manage expectations effectively are more likely to retain investor confidence throughout the business cycle. Those that overpromise, conceal problems or deflect blame gradually lose credibility. Once trust is lost, it is often difficult to regain.

The responsibilities of an IR consultant therefore extend far beyond administrative and public relations functions. A professional IR consultant is, in essence, a strategic adviser to the board and senior management. To perform this role effectively, an IR consultant requires a sound understanding of business strategy, accounting, finance, valuation, economics and investor behaviour, together with the ability to communicate clearly and persuasively.

In many respects, the skills and knowledge required of an IR consultant closely resemble those of an equity analyst. The relationship between the two is best viewed as two sides of the same coin – one provides information, while the other evaluates and interprets it. IR consultants who understand how analysts think are better equipped to anticipate questions, provide meaningful answers and communicate a company's investment case more effectively – not only to analysts but also to the wider investment community.

This book approaches IR through the eyes of an analyst. It begins by examining the mental models that shape analytical thinking before exploring how businesses create value, how financial models are constructed, how companies are valued and, finally, how these elements come together to form a clear and compelling investment proposition.

Whether you are new to IR or seeking to deepen your understanding of the profession, I hope this book encourages you to see IR from a different perspective. By learning to think like an analyst, you will discover that IR and equity research are not opposing disciplines, but complementary ones. The journey begins by understanding how analysts think, for only by seeing the business through their eyes can IR professionals communicate what truly matters to the market.

Chapter 1

The Mental Model

The role of IR is not simply about communicating with the market. It is about communicating in a way that the market understands, appreciates and trusts. To do that effectively, an IR consultant must first understand how the investment community thinks.

This chapter introduces the analyst's mental model. It explains their roles, how they think, what they look for, and how they communicate investment ideas. Once you understand this, you will find it much easier to answer their questions, prepare management for investor meetings and position your company more effectively.

Understanding the Analysts

The primary role of an equity analyst is to understand a company's business, estimate its intrinsic value and make recommendations to investors on whether to buy, hold or sell its shares.

Analysts can be grouped according to the role they play within the investment industry. The first distinction an IR consultant should understand is between buy-side and sell-side analysts:

Buy-side analysts work for investment institutions such as fund managers, insurance companies, pension funds and family offices. Their research is prepared for internal use to support investment decisions made by their own organisation. Because their work is proprietary, it is rarely made available to the public.

Sell-side analysts work for investment banks and stockbroking firms. Their research is distributed to clients and is intended to help investors make informed investment decisions. Besides publishing research reports, sell-side analysts also present their investment ideas through client meetings, conferences and roadshows. As a result, they are often the analysts whom IR consultants interact with most frequently.

Analysts may also specialise in different areas of research:

Sector analysts focus on specific industries such as technology, healthcare, banking or property. By covering several companies within the same sector, they develop a deep understanding of industry trends, competitive dynamics and valuation benchmarks. Their work helps investors compare companies and identify the strongest investment opportunities within an industry.

Economists study macroeconomic factors such as economic growth, inflation, interest rates, exchange rates and government policies. Their research helps investors understand how changes in the economy may affect corporate earnings and market conditions.

Strategists take a broader view of the capital markets. They analyse market valuations, investor sentiment, fund flows and asset allocation to determine where investment opportunities are likely to emerge. While economists focus on the economy and sector analysts focus on individual industries, strategists help investors decide which markets, sectors or asset classes deserve greater attention.

Research houses that the analysts work for can also be distinguished according to the type of investors they serve:

Institutional research houses primarily cater to professional investors such as fund managers and insurance companies. Their reports are usually more detailed, with greater emphasis on financial modelling, valuation and investment risks.

Retail research houses write mainly for individual investors. Their reports tend to use simpler language and focus on the key investment message rather than technical details. While the style of writing may differ, the underlying analysis should remain the same. The difference lies not in the quality of the research, but in how the information is presented to suit the intended audience.

Understanding the Research Reports

One of the best ways to understand an analyst is to study the reports they write. Although research reports differ in style from one institution to another, most contain the same core elements. They usually begin with a recommendation and a target price, followed by a short investment summary. The summary is often presented in three concise bullet points that explain why the analyst believes the stock is attractive or unattractive. The report then provides supporting analysis, financial forecasts and the valuation used to derive the target price.

This structure is deliberate. Most fund managers and professional investors do not have the time to read every report in detail. They want to understand the investment conclusion quickly before deciding whether to study the report further. The headline tells them the key message. The target price tells them the analyst's estimate of fair value. The three bullet points summarise the investment case. The rest of the report provides the evidence supporting those conclusions.

There is an important lesson here for every IR consultant. A good investment pitch should follow the same principle. Start with the key message. Explain why it matters. Support it with evidence. Do not force your audience to search for the conclusion.

Price Targets and Catalysts

One of the most widely quoted figures in an analyst's report is the target price. Investors often compare the target price with the current share price to estimate the potential upside or downside of an investment. While the target price is important, many investors focus too heavily on the number itself rather than the assumptions and catalysts that underpin it.

A target price is usually the analyst's estimate of the company's fair value based on a set of assumptions. These assumptions are derived from the analyst's understanding of the business, financial forecasts and the valuation methodology used. If any of these assumptions change, the target price will also change. More importantly, a target price is only a number. It does not explain how or when the market will recognise that value. This is where catalysts become important.

A catalyst is a trigger event that causes investors to reassess their expectations of a company's future performance and, consequently, its value. Positive catalysts include stronger-than-expected earnings, major contract wins, successful product launches, mergers and acquisitions, industry recovery, favourable government policies and improvements in corporate governance. Conversely, earnings disappointments, regulatory actions or the loss of key customers may cause investors to lower their expectations and reassess the company's value.

Identifying catalysts is an important part of an analyst's work because value, or more specifically the target price, rarely drives share prices on its own. A company may remain undervalued for years if there is no reason for investors to change their perception. Likewise, an overvalued company may continue to trade at a premium until investors begin to question its outlook. For this reason, analysts do not simply ask what a company is worth. They also ask what is likely to change the market's perception of that value.

The same principle applies to IR. A good IR consultant does not merely communicate past achievements. They also help investors understand the future developments that are likely to influence the company's growth, earnings and valuation. By identifying and communicating meaningful catalysts, IR consultants help the market understand not only what the company is worth, but also why that value may eventually be recognised.

Understanding the Thought Process

To many IR consultants, analysts seem to ask an endless stream of questions during meetings. In reality, these questions are rarely random. Every question is asked to fill a gap in their thought process.

An analyst begins by understanding how the company creates value through its business model. They then translate that understanding into a financial model to forecast future earnings before applying an appropriate valuation model to estimate what the company is worth. Every question they ask helps them complete one part of this process.

For example, an analyst may ask whether a particular source of revenue is recurring or one-off. This is not simply a question about revenue. It helps determine whether future earnings are sustainable and whether today's profits can be projected into future years.

Likewise, questions about customer concentration, pricing, operating margins or capital expenditure are not isolated questions. They are inputs into the analyst's business model, financial model or valuation model.

Once you understand where each question fits within this framework, analyst meetings become much easier to navigate. Instead of responding to isolated questions, you begin to recognise the underlying objective behind them, allowing you to provide clearer answers and anticipate the next question before it is asked.

Understanding the Communication Habits

Understanding the analyst's thought process is only half the picture. Equally important is understanding how that thought process is communicated. The techniques used by analysts in their reports and presentations are not arbitrary. They are designed to present investment ideas in a manner that is logical, evidence-based and easy for investors to understand.

Pitching With Facts

When it comes to pitching, one common characteristic of professional analysts is the way they present their ideas using facts. Analysts rarely rely on descriptive words such as "strong", "excellent" or "promising". While these words may sound persuasive, they merely express the writer's opinion and provide little evidence to support the argument. Instead, analysts present facts that readers can verify for themselves.

For example, it is more convincing to say that revenue grew by 20% than to describe the company's growth as "strong". Likewise, saying that the company has a 35% market share conveys much more information than simply calling it a market leader. Facts allow readers to reach their own conclusions. Opinions ask readers to accept the writer's judgement.

The same principle applies to IR. Whenever possible, replace adjectives with measurable facts. Instead of saying the company has a "strong balance sheet", explain that it has a net cash position of S$500 million. Rather than describing demand as "robust", state that the order book has reached a record S$2 billion. The numbers speak for themselves.

This does not mean adjectives should never be used. They can help improve the flow and readability of a presentation. However, they should support the facts rather than replace them. Facts build credibility. Credibility builds trust. Trust, ultimately, is the foundation of effective IR.

Keeping It Concise

A common mistake made by new IR consultants is to assume that more information leads to a stronger pitch. In reality, the opposite is often true. Professional investors are busy. They appreciate information that is organised, relevant and easy to understand. Flooding an audience with information often dilutes the main message rather than strengthens it.

Experienced analysts often use the **elevator pitch** to sell their ideas to investors. An elevator pitch is a brief 30- to 60-second summary that communicates the essence of an investment idea. It is not intended to explain every detail. Rather, its objective is to capture the listener's attention and generate sufficient interest for a deeper discussion.

Developing an effective elevator pitch is also an excellent discipline for organising your own thoughts. It forces you to identify the few factors that truly matter and remove everything else. If you struggle to explain an investment idea clearly within a minute, it is often a sign that your own thinking is not yet clear. Before trying to convince others, you must first convince yourself.

Being concise does not mean leaving out important information. It means removing information that is not important to the point you are trying to make. Once your audience understands the key message, you can always provide more details if they are interested.

Professionalism and Ethics

Like IR consultants, analysts are constantly exposed to market rumours, speculation and, on occasion, material non-public information. The way they handle such information determines not only their personal reputation, but also the credibility of their organisation and the confidence of the investment community.

Rumours are common in the capital markets. Some eventually prove to be true, while many are inaccurate or deliberately misleading. Professional analysts do not treat rumours as facts. Instead, they verify information through reliable sources before incorporating it into their analysis or reports. Likewise, IR consultants should avoid confirming, denying or commenting on market rumours unless the company has made an official announcement. Responding carelessly to speculation may create confusion, damage credibility, or expose the company to regulatory risks.

An even greater responsibility arises when dealing with insider information. Material non-public information refers to information that has not been released to the market but is likely to influence an investor's decision if it becomes known. Examples include unpublished financial results, major acquisitions, significant contract wins or changes in senior management. Such information must never be selectively disclosed to analysts or investors before it is announced publicly. Doing so may constitute insider trading or selective disclosure, both of which undermine market integrity and investor confidence.

Professionalism is not measured by how much information an analyst or IR consultant possesses. It is measured by how responsibly that information is handled. Credibility is built over years through honesty, discipline and consistent ethical behaviour. Once lost, it is difficult to regain.

For an IR consultant, trust is one of the company's most valuable assets. Every meeting, every presentation and every conversation with the investment community should reinforce that trust. Always communicate facts rather than rumours, disclose information fairly and consistently, and remember that long-term credibility is far more valuable than any short-term gain.

Chapter 2

The Business Model

Before an analyst studies a company's financial statements, builds a financial model or determines a target price, they first need to understand the business itself. The reason is simple. Financial statements describe what has happened in the past, but the business model explains why it happened and whether it is likely to happen again.

A business model shows how a company creates value for its shareholders. It explains what the company sells, who its customers are, how it generates revenue, what costs it incurs, how it earns profits and generates cash flow, and ultimately, how it derives its valuation. Every figure reported in the financial statements is a consequence of the underlying business model. Without understanding the business, the numbers have little meaning.

The business model also has important implications for the rest of an analyst's work. Once the business model is understood, the analyst can identify the key drivers of revenue, costs and profitability before translating them into a financial model. Those forecasts then become the basis for selecting an appropriate valuation methodology and determining the company's target price. Finally, the strengths of the business model form the foundation of the company's positioning and investment pitch. In other words, every subsequent chapter in this book begins with the business model.

The Diversity of Business Models

No two companies are exactly alike. Even companies operating in the same industry may have very different business models. They may sell different products, serve different customers, compete using different strategies or operate under different cost structures. Their management teams may adopt different growth strategies, capital structures or dividend policies. These differences ultimately affect the company's earnings, cash flow, risk profile and valuation.

Consider the pharmaceutical industry. Medicines are generally regarded as essential products, making demand relatively stable regardless of economic conditions. At first glance, this suggests that pharmaceutical companies should enjoy stable earnings and defensive valuations. However, this is only part of the story.

A pharmaceutical company that owns patented drugs may enjoy stronger pricing power and higher profit margins because competitors are prevented from producing the same medicine. Once the patents expire, however, generic manufacturers may enter the market and cause prices and margins to decline sharply. Another pharmaceutical company may focus entirely on generic drugs, where competition is intense but demand remains relatively stable. Although both companies operate in the same industry, their earnings quality, growth prospects and valuations may differ significantly because their business models are different.

The business model may also be influenced by factors beyond the company's operations. A highly geared company may be more sensitive to changes in interest rates than a debt-free competitor. A company that exports most of its products may be exposed to fluctuations in foreign exchange rates. Different accounting policies may affect reported earnings, while changes in government regulations can alter industry profitability almost overnight.

For this reason, analysts rarely classify companies simply by industry. Instead, they seek to understand the unique characteristics that make each business different. Every company is a combination of operational, financial and external factors. The possible combinations are almost limitless, making every business model unique.

Identifying the Business Model

Given the wide variety of business models, where should an analyst begin?

Surprisingly, many analysts do not begin with the business. They begin with the stock. Before understanding how a company operates, analysts often form an initial view of how the market perceives the company. Is it a growth stock? A defensive stock? A dividend stock? A cyclical stock? A recovery story? Or a speculative investment?

This initial positioning is not intended to reach a conclusion. Instead, it provides a working hypothesis. The analyst then studies the business model to determine whether the evidence supports that positioning. Suppose the market regards a company as a growth stock. The analyst would expect to find characteristics such as expanding markets, increasing demand, strong earnings growth and opportunities to reinvest capital at attractive returns. If these characteristics are absent, the market's positioning may be incorrect.

Likewise, if a company is regarded as a defensive stock, the analyst would expect to see stable demand, recurring revenue, resilient margins and relatively predictable earnings. Again, the business model should support the positioning.

Rather than memorising hundreds of different business models, experienced analysts work backwards. They begin with the market's perception, identify the characteristics associated with that positioning and then determine whether the company's business model supports those characteristics. This approach allows analysts to understand even unfamiliar businesses quickly and systematically.

Common Stock Positioning

Although every company is unique, most listed companies can broadly be associated with one or more common investment themes:

Growth stocks are expected to deliver above-average earnings growth, usually because they operate in expanding markets, introduce innovative products or continue to gain market share. Investors are often willing to pay higher valuation multiples for companies that can sustain this growth.

Defensive stocks generate relatively stable earnings regardless of economic conditions. Businesses that provide essential goods and services, such as healthcare, utilities and consumer staples, are often regarded as defensive because demand remains relatively resilient during economic downturns.

Dividend stocks are valued for their ability to generate consistent cash flow and distribute a meaningful portion of their earnings to shareholders. Mature businesses with stable operations and limited capital expenditure requirements often fall into this category.

Cyclical stocks experience earnings that rise and fall with the business cycle. Industries such as property, construction, commodities and shipping are influenced by economic activity, causing profits to fluctuate significantly over time.

Recovery stocks are companies whose earnings have been temporarily affected by operational problems, industry downturns or economic shocks. Investors purchase these companies in anticipation of improving business conditions and recovering profitability.

Speculative stocks generally have uncertain earnings or business models but possess the potential for significant future growth. These companies often attract investors willing to accept higher risks in exchange for potentially higher returns.

More details on these investment themes are available at the end of this book.

Finding the Supporting Evidence

The next step is to seek evidence to support the hypothesis. This is where analysts differ from storytellers. A storyteller starts with a conclusion and looks for reasons to support it. An analyst starts with a hypothesis and looks for evidence that either supports or contradicts it. If the evidence contradicts the original hypothesis, the analyst changes the conclusion rather than ignores the facts.

For an IR consultant, this distinction is equally important. Good positioning is never about inventing a story. It is about discovering the strongest investment case that is already supported by the company's business model. The evidence usually comes from four broad sources: the business, the financial statements, the management strategy and the external environment.

The Business

The first source of information is the business itself. Analysts begin by understanding what the company sells, who its customers are and how it generates revenue. They study the company's products and services, customer base, competitors, suppliers and competitive advantages. They also examine whether demand is recurring or one-off, whether the company has pricing power and whether there are barriers that prevent competitors from entering the market.

Much of this information can be obtained from the company's annual report, investor presentations, corporate website and product catalogues. Analysts often supplement this with factory visits, store visits, conversations with suppliers and customers, competitor research and industry reports.

The Financial Statements

While the business explains how the company operates, the financial statements show how the business model is translated into numbers. Many beginners treat the income statement, balance sheet and cash flow statement as accounting reports. Analysts see them differently. They view the financial statements as a numerical description of the business model.

The income statement reveals how the company earns its profits. Revenue shows the scale of the business, while gross profit margins indicate pricing power and cost competitiveness. Operating expenses reveal where the company spends its money. For example, a retailer may incur significant rental and labour expenses because of its physical store network. A technology company may spend heavily on research and development. A property developer may report substantial interest expenses because of its higher borrowings. These expenses often reveal more about the business model than the profits themselves.

The balance sheet explains how the business is financed and operated. Asset-heavy businesses such as airlines, manufacturers and infrastructure companies usually own significant amounts of property, plant and equipment. Retailers often carry large inventories but may enjoy negative working capital because customers pay immediately while suppliers are paid later. Property companies typically operate with higher gearing because debt is used to finance land acquisition and development. Each balance sheet tells a story about how the business operates.

The cash flow statement completes the picture. It shows whether accounting profits are converted into cash. Some companies report strong earnings but generate weak operating cash flow because profits are tied up in receivables or inventory. Others consistently convert earnings into cash, reflecting a healthier business model. Capital expenditure also provides useful insights. High capital expenditure may indicate expansion and future growth, while lower capital expenditure may suggest a mature business with stronger free cash flow and greater dividend-paying capacity.

Rather than studying each financial statement separately, analysts connect them together. The numbers should support the business model. If they do not, further investigation is required.

The Management Strategy

A business model does not remain static. It evolves with management's strategy. Analysts therefore spend considerable time understanding management's plans. Are they expanding into new markets? Launching new products? Building additional production capacity? Improving operational efficiency? Reducing costs? Acquiring new businesses?

Management's strategy provides important clues about the company's future direction. An aggressive expansion plan may reinforce a growth investment thesis by creating new revenue opportunities and accelerating future earnings growth. Conversely, it may require significant capital expenditure or acquisitions, placing pressure on cash flow and reducing the company's ability to sustain high dividend payouts. Similarly, a cost rationalisation programme may strengthen a recovery thesis by improving margins, while signing long-term customer contracts may reinforce a defensive positioning by making future earnings more predictable.

Nevertheless, experienced analysts do not rely solely on management's plans. They compare management's plans with its track record, available resources and financial capacity to determine whether those plans are realistic and achievable. A credible strategy is one that is supported by evidence, not merely ambition.

The External Environment

Finally, no business operates in isolation. The external environment can have a significant influence on a company's performance, regardless of how well it is managed. Macroeconomic conditions, interest rates, exchange rates, commodity prices, government regulations, demographic trends and technological developments may all affect the business model.

For some companies, these external factors become the key earnings drivers. Property developers are highly sensitive to interest rates. Airlines are affected by fuel prices. Exporters may benefit from a weaker domestic currency. Pharmaceutical companies depend on regulatory approvals and patent protection.

Connecting the Dots

The objective of analysing a business model is not to collect as much information as possible. It is to identify the few factors that truly drive the business. Every company has hundreds of operating statistics, financial ratios and industry data points. Many are interesting. Only a handful determine the company's future earnings and ultimately its valuation.

For an analyst, understanding the business model is therefore more than learning about products and services. It is the foundation upon which the financial model is built. Once the key business drivers have been identified, they can be translated into financial drivers, allowing future earnings to be forecast and the company to be valued.

The same thought process applies to IR. Effective positioning does not begin with marketing or storytelling. It begins with understanding the business. The business model drives the financial model. The financial model underpins the valuation. The valuation shapes the investment proposition. Only when these pieces fit together can a company be positioned credibly and convincingly to investors.

Chapter 3

The Financial Model

If the business model explains how a company generates its earnings, the financial model translates that business model into numbers by forecasting its future financial performance. Analysts spend much of their time building financial models because investment decisions are based on future earnings rather than historical results. Investors buy shares for what a company is expected to earn, not for what it earned last year.

A financial model is simply a structured method of forecasting a company's future financial performance. It translates the business model into numbers by identifying the key earnings drivers, making reasonable assumptions and projecting future revenue, costs and profits. Depending on the analyst's objectives, the model may also forecast the balance sheet and cash flow statement.

For an IR consultant, the financial model is equally important. It explains why analysts ask certain questions, why they focus on specific business drivers and why seemingly small changes in assumptions can have a significant impact on earnings forecasts and valuation.

The Mindset

A financial model is often described as a forecasting tool. In reality, it is simply a calculator that produces forecasts based on the assumptions fed into it. Like any calculator, the quality of its output depends entirely on the quality of its inputs. Analysts often summarise this principle as "Garbage In, Garbage Out". No matter how sophisticated a spreadsheet may appear, unrealistic assumptions will inevitably produce unrealistic forecasts.

A common mistake is to become either overly optimistic or overly pessimistic. Some analysts adopt aggressive assumptions because they share management's optimism or wish to maintain a good relationship with the company. Others deliberately adopt overly cautious assumptions to play it safe. Both approaches are flawed and are more likely to produce forecasts that miss the mark.

The objective of financial modelling is neither to be bullish nor conservative. It is to produce the most probable forecast based on the evidence available at that point in time. This gives any investment decision based on the model and its underlying assumptions the highest probability of being correct. Good analysts remain objective. When new evidence emerges, they will revise their assumptions accordingly.

Exploring the Scenarios

Experienced analysts rarely rely on a single forecast. The future is uncertain, and there is often more than one possible outcome. Analysts use their "calculator" to project different outcomes under different sets of assumptions. This allows them to explore various possibilities, understand the impact of changing business conditions and evaluate the risks and rewards of an investment. More importantly, when new information becomes available, analysts can quickly react to changes and not be completely caught off guard.

The most common scenarios are the Best Case, Bull Case, Base Case, Bear Case and Worst Case:

Best Case represents the upper limit of what a company could reasonably achieve. It assumes the best possible outcome for every major earnings driver, such as exceptionally strong demand, higher selling prices, faster expansion and greater operating efficiency. Unlike the Bull Case, the Best Case deliberately pushes the assumptions towards their practical limits to determine the maximum value that can be justified by the underlying business.

The Best Case therefore serves as an important reality check. A good example was the valuation of SpaceX before its anticipated IPO in 2026. Some analysts concluded that the implied market valuation had exceeded their Best Case estimates based on the company's projected earnings and cash flows. This did not necessarily mean that SpaceX was a poor company. Rather, it suggested that investors were paying too much for future possibilities that could not be justified under these analysts' most optimistic assumptions. The Best Case therefore helps analysts establish the upper boundary of a company's valuation and identify situations where market expectations may have become unrealistically optimistic.

Bull Case assumes favourable developments for the key earnings drivers, but within realistic and achievable limits. Revenue may grow at an unusually strong pace, margins may improve, or expansion plans may be executed ahead of schedule. Analysts often use the Bull Case to estimate the potential upside if management executes well and market conditions remain supportive.

Base Case represents the most probable outcome based on the information available at the time. It lies somewhere between the optimistic and pessimistic scenarios, but not necessarily at the midpoint. Every assumption used in the Base Case reflects what the analyst believes is the most likely outcome for the company's key earnings drivers. The resulting earnings forecast and valuation are typically used to derive the target price. At the same time, analysts continue to monitor developments that could shift the company towards the Bull Case or the Bear Case.

Bear Case is a less negative scenario than the Worst Case. It assumes weaker business conditions that remain realistic, such as slower growth, softer margins or temporary operational setbacks. Analysts use the Bear Case to estimate the downside risk if the business underperforms expectations without facing an extreme crisis.

Worst Case is the opposite extreme of Best Case. It assumes the most adverse outcome for the key earnings drivers, such as significantly weaker demand, falling selling prices, rising costs or severe operational disruptions. In some cases, analysts may incorporate a black swan event – a rare and highly unpredictable event with a major impact on the company or the broader economy. The Worst Case therefore serves as a stress test. If the company can survive under these assumptions, analysts gain greater confidence in its financial resilience.

In conclusion, scenario analysis is not about predicting the future with certainty. It is about preparing for different possibilities, understanding how changes in key assumptions affect the investment case and making better-informed decisions as new information emerges. Ultimately, the value of a financial model lies not in producing a single forecast, but in helping analysts understand the full range of possible outcomes.

Managing the Variances

Every earnings announcement provides an opportunity to compare the model against reality. The differences, known as variances, reveal which assumptions were correct and which require revision.

The first variance that analysts usually examine is the reported net profit, commonly referred to as an "earnings beat" when results exceed expectations, or an "earnings miss" when they fall short. Depending on the outcome, such surprises may have a significant impact on the company's valuation. This is because they suggest that one or more assumptions within the financial model are no longer valid, or that the momentum of key earnings drivers – such as revenue growth, margins or operating costs – has changed in either magnitude or direction.

However, an accurate earnings forecast does not necessarily mean that the underlying assumptions are correct. In many cases, changes in different earnings drivers offset one another. For example, stronger-than-expected revenue may be offset by weaker-than-expected profit margins, resulting in a net profit that matches the original forecast. Although the bottom line appears accurate, the underlying assumptions have changed. Once these assumptions are updated, the financial model may still point to a revision in future earnings forecasts and, consequently, the company's valuation.

Occasionally, reported earnings may also be distorted by one-off items that do not reflect the company's underlying operating performance. These may include gains from asset disposals, fair value revaluations, impairment charges or restructuring provisions. In some situations, non-operating gains may temporarily offset weaker operating performance. At other times, management may recognise large provisions or impairments during a strong financial year to clean up the balance sheet and create a stronger buffer for future periods.

Experienced analysts are generally able to identify these adjustments and will revise their assumptions based on the company's core or adjusted earnings instead of the reported figures.

For an IR consultant, understanding these variances is just as important as understanding the financial model itself. When analysts question a company's results, they are rarely interested only in whether earnings beat or missed expectations. More importantly, they want to know **which assumptions changed, why they changed** and **whether those changes are temporary or permanent**. The ability to explain these differences clearly helps management maintain credibility and enables investors to update their expectations with greater confidence.

Building the Model

Financial models may differ from one analyst to another, but the overall process is remarkably similar.

Step 1 – Copy the Historical Financial Statements

Every financial model begins with historical data. The simplest approach is to reproduce the company's published financial statements in the Excel spreadsheet using the same reporting format wherever possible. This makes it easier to update the model after every quarterly or annual results announcement while reducing the risk of transcription errors. Historical data also provides the foundation for identifying trends, calculating ratios and understanding how the business has evolved over time.

Step 2 – Identify the Key Drivers

Once the historical data has been entered, the next step is to identify the key variables that drive the business. Analysts usually begin with the largest components of the income statement because they have the greatest influence on earnings. Revenue and cost of goods sold (or gross profit margin) are often the most important drivers. However, every business is different, and certain income or expense items below the gross profit line may play a more significant role depending on the business model. For a property developer, interest expense can be a critical earnings driver because of its highly geared balance sheet. For a retailer, rental and labour costs are often the major operating expenses.

This is where the understanding gained from the business model becomes invaluable. The business model explains what drives the financial variables and, ultimately, the company's earnings. Instead of forecasting the financial statements directly, experienced analysts first forecast the underlying business drivers. For example, the revenue of a hotel owner depends largely on three key drivers: the number of available rooms, the average occupancy rate and the average room rate. Likewise, the revenue of a construction company is driven by the size of its order book, the construction progress of its projects and the accounting principles governing how much revenue can be recognised at each stage of completion. Once these business drivers have been estimated, the corresponding financial figures can be calculated systematically.

It is also important to understand how the income statement, balance sheet and cash flow statement are linked. These three financial statements should never be analysed in isolation, as a change in one statement often affects the others. For a property developer, interest expense cannot be forecast without first estimating the borrowings on its balance sheet. As projects are completed, borrowings may be repaid, reducing future interest expense and improving profitability. The financial model therefore needs to capture these relationships to produce realistic forecasts.

Similarly, for technology companies, part of the development expenditure may be capitalised on the balance sheet and amortised through the income statement over its estimated useful life. If the technology becomes obsolete earlier than expected, the remaining carrying cost may have to be written off through an impairment charge. Although these amortisation and impairment charges reduce reported earnings, they do not involve an immediate cash outflow. Analysts who place greater emphasis on operating cash flow will therefore distinguish between accounting earnings in the income statement and cash generation in the cash flow statement when assessing the company's financial performance.

Ultimately, every figure in the financial statements should be traceable back to an underlying business activity. The better an analyst understands the relationship between the business model and the financial statements, the easier it becomes to identify the assumptions that truly matter. Financial models do not forecast financial statements; they forecast business drivers, with the financial statements becoming the mathematical outcome of those assumptions.

Step 3 – Analyse the Trends

Once the key drivers have been identified, the next step is to analyse how they have behaved over time. Is revenue accelerating or slowing? Are profit margins improving or deteriorating? Has operating efficiency increased? Are costs rising faster than sales? Historical trends often provide useful clues about how the business is evolving and form the basis for forecasting future performance.

When analysing trends, analysts always work from the underlying business drivers rather than relying solely on the reported financial figures. Earnings drivers are often influenced by one or more business drivers, each with its own trend. For example, the revenue of a commodity producer may be growing because commodity prices are rising, production volume is increasing or both. Although the reported revenue may show a single upward trend, the underlying drivers may be moving in different directions. Identifying and separating these drivers allows analysts to understand what is truly driving the business and make more reliable forecasts.

Segmentation is therefore an important part of trend analysis. Breaking down revenue, costs or profits by product, business segment or geographical market often reveals patterns that are hidden within the consolidated financial statements. Different segments may be growing at different rates, facing different cost pressures or responding differently to changes in the economic environment. Understanding these differences enables analysts to identify the key drivers more accurately.

Another important consideration is the impact of one-off items, which can distort the underlying trend. These may include gains from asset disposals, impairment charges, restructuring costs, fair value adjustments or other non-recurring items. Analysts therefore separate these items from the company's core operating performance to obtain a clearer picture of its sustainable earnings. Forecasts should generally be based on recurring earnings rather than temporary accounting events.

Finally, historical trends should serve as a guide rather than a prediction of the future. Trends can change as business conditions evolve, competition intensifies, management strategies shift or unexpected events occur. The purpose of trend analysis is therefore not to extrapolate the past mechanically, but to understand why a trend exists and whether it is likely to continue.

Step 4 – Making the Assumptions

Forecasting begins with assumptions. The challenge is that the future is uncertain, and complete information is rarely available. Analysts therefore need to make reasonable assumptions using the best evidence available.

One common approach is to extrapolate historical trends. If a company's sales volume has grown consistently at around 10% per year, historical growth may provide a reasonable starting point, provided the underlying business conditions remain unchanged.

Internal information supplied by the company can also improve the quality of forecasts. Management guidance, order books, production capacity, operating statistics and expansion plans often provide useful insights into future performance. Such information is particularly valuable because it reflects the latest developments within the business that may not yet be visible in the historical financial statements.

External information is equally important. Industry reports, government statistics, economic indicators, commodity prices and competitor performance all help analysts understand the broader operating environment and refine their assumptions.

Sometimes, relationships between variables can provide useful forecasting clues. For example, the average selling price of a gold mining company is closely linked to gold prices, while the order book of a construction company often tracks industry demand and construction activity. Within the company, certain variables can also move in tandem. Selling and distribution expenses generally increase with sales because higher revenue usually requires more advertising, sales commissions and logistics support. Understanding these relationships allows analysts to forecast one variable based on another, resulting in a more logical and consistent financial model.

Not all information carries the same weight. Analysts always place greater reliance on objective and verifiable evidence than on opinions or aspirations. For example, a signed order book provides stronger support than management's optimism about future demand. Likewise, actual operating statistics generally carry more weight than broad market expectations. The stronger the evidence supporting an assumption, the greater the confidence in the forecast.

Despite all these tools, forecasting is never an exact science. Occasionally, analysts simply have to make their best judgement based on incomplete information – what is often referred to as a "finger-in-the-air" estimate. This does not mean the estimate is arbitrary. Rather, it reflects a professional judgement after considering all the available evidence. As new information emerges, these assumptions should be reviewed and refined accordingly.

Ultimately, every assumption should answer one simple question: "Why do I believe this number is reasonable?" If the assumption cannot be supported by logic or evidence, it probably needs to be reconsidered.

Step 5 – Continuous Review

A financial model is never complete. Every quarterly result, annual report, management briefing and industry development provides new information that may affect the model. Experienced analysts review and update their forecasts continuously.

Updating the numbers is only part of the process. More importantly, analysts revisit the assumptions behind those numbers. Has management changed its guidance? Has demand strengthened or weakened? Have industry conditions improved? Has a key driver behaved differently from expectations?

Over time, this process of reviewing assumptions, measuring variances and refining forecasts produces a deeper understanding of both the company and its business model. A financial model should therefore be viewed as a living document rather than a static spreadsheet. Its greatest value lies not in the numbers it produces, but in the disciplined thinking that goes into building and continuously improving it.

Chapter 4

The Valuation Model

If the business model explains how a company generates its earnings, and the financial model forecasts those earnings, the valuation model determines what those future earnings are worth today.

Valuation is one of the most misunderstood aspects of investing. Many beginners think there is a single "correct" value for every company. In reality, valuation is an estimate based on assumptions. Different analysts can value the same company differently because they choose different valuation models, different peer groups and different assumptions. The objective of valuation is therefore not to determine an exact value of a company. Rather, it is to estimate a reasonable range of values based on the information available at that point in time.

The diversity of business models means every company creates value differently and therefore needs to be valued differently. Some companies derive most of their value from earnings, others from their assets, while some are better understood through their cash flows.

Earnings-Based Valuation

Earnings-based valuation is the most widely used valuation approach because, ultimately, investors buy companies for their ability to generate profits.

Characteristics

This approach works best when earnings possess characteristics that contribute to a single objective – predictability.

Visibility. Analysts need sufficient information about the future to forecast earnings with reasonable confidence. Consider a company with only one month of confirmed orders and no indication of whether additional contracts will be secured thereafter. Without visibility, how should future earnings be projected? More importantly, how can those earnings be valued? The less visible the future, the greater the forecasting risk. This is why companies with higher earnings visibility often command higher valuation multiples. Greater visibility reduces uncertainty, and investors are generally willing to pay more for certainty.

Stability. Businesses with highly erratic profits are difficult to value using earnings multiples because one year's earnings may not represent the company's true earning power. This is particularly true for companies with cyclical earnings, such as mining companies, or businesses with lumpy earnings, such as property developers and construction companies. In these situations, a single year's earnings may fluctuate significantly even though the underlying value of the business has changed very little.

Trends. The earnings should exhibit a meaningful trend. Investors are generally willing to pay higher valuation multiples for companies that can consistently grow their earnings over time, and lower multiples for companies whose earnings are stagnant, declining or highly volatile.

Overall, the more strongly a company exhibits these characteristics – visibility, stability and trend – the more suitable it is for using earnings-based valuation. Companies that commonly possess these characteristics include those in the manufacturing, consumer, healthcare, technology, services and most industrial sectors.

Methodologies

The most widely used earnings-based valuation method is the Price-to-Earnings (P/E) ratio. It is calculated by dividing the share price by the earnings per share or, equivalently, the company's market capitalisation by its net profit. It measures how many times investors are willing to pay for one year's earnings.

The multiple reflects a balance between risk and return. Companies with lower perceived risks, stronger earnings visibility and higher expected growth generally trade at higher P/E multiples because investors are willing to pay more for greater certainty and better long-term prospects.

Historical P/E. This ratio uses the previous financial year's reported net profit as the basis for earnings. An expanding historical P/E usually points to improving growth expectations, while a contracting historical P/E often reflects weakening expectations. As such, it provides a useful indication of how much future growth the market has already priced into the stock.

Trailing P/E. This ratio, more commonly known as the Trailing Twelve Months (TTM) P/E, uses earnings from the most recent twelve months. Although similar to the Historical P/E, it is generally more responsive because it reflects the company's latest reported performance. Like the Historical P/E, it is useful for tracking how market expectations change over time.

The following chart illustrates the relationship between ST Engineering's Trailing P/E and its expected twelve-month earnings growth between 1998 and 2007.

Chart 4.1: ST Engineering Trailing P/E versus Expected Earnings Growth

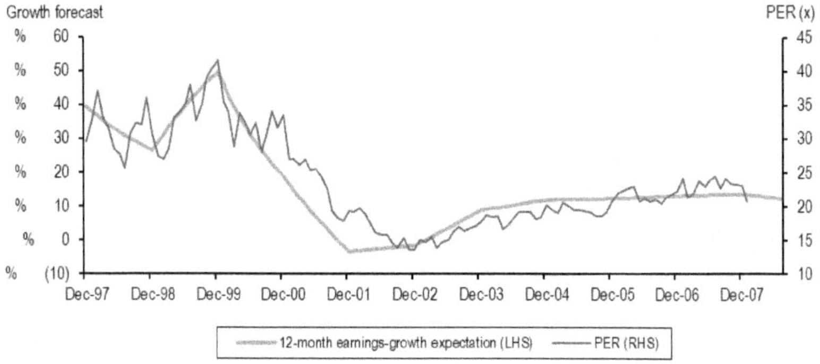

Source: Bloomberg

The positive correlation is clear. As growth expectations increased, the Trailing P/E also expanded. Conversely, when growth expectations weakened, the valuation multiple contracted. This observation is one of the main reasons why I personally prefer using the Trailing P/E. If the earnings forecast is correct, history suggests that the market often adjusts the valuation multiple in line with changing growth expectations. In other words, forecasting earnings accurately frequently leads to a reasonable estimate of both the appropriate P/E multiple and the company's valuation.

Forward P/E. This ratio uses forecast earnings instead of historical earnings. Since future growth has already been incorporated into the earnings forecast, the valuation multiple should, in theory, remain relatively stable. In practice, however, the Forward P/E is anything but stable.

Unlike Historical or Trailing P/E, whose earnings are fixed using reported historical figures, forecast earnings are constantly revised as analysts update their assumptions based on new information. As a result, even if the share price remains unchanged, the Forward P/E can fluctuate simply because the earnings forecast has changed.

The usefulness of the Forward P/E therefore depends not only on the quality and consistency of the underlying earnings forecasts, but also on the efficiency with which the market incorporates new information into the share price. In an efficient market, revisions to earnings expectations are quickly reflected in the share price, allowing the Forward P/E to remain relatively stable. However, if the market is slow to react, changes in earnings forecasts may not be immediately matched by movements in the share price, causing the Forward P/E to fluctuate over a wider range.

PEG Ratio. Another commonly used earnings-based valuation model is the Price-Earnings-to-Growth (PEG) ratio. It relates a company's P/E ratio to its expected earnings growth, providing a simple measure of how much investors are paying for future growth.

Every P/E ratio reflects growth, albeit in different ways. Historical and Trailing P/E express growth through changes in the valuation multiple. Forward P/E incorporates growth directly into the forecast earnings. The PEG ratio, however, implicitly assumes a proportional relationship between P/E and expected earnings growth. In my view, this is the model's greatest weakness.

Taken literally, the implication becomes unrealistic. A company with an expected earnings growth approaching zero would imply a negligible P/E multiple, while a company with negative earnings growth would imply a negative P/E multiple. Clearly, this is not how markets behave. Returning to the ST Engineering example, the P/E remained at around 15 times even when expected earnings growth approached zero. The market continued to assign substantial value to the company despite the absence of near-term growth.

There is undoubtedly a relationship between P/E and growth. Faster-growing companies generally command higher P/E multiples than slower-growing companies. However, that relationship is correlational rather than proportional. As a result, the PEG ratio has severe limitations and should only be applied with a clear understanding of its underlying assumptions.

P/S Ratio. Not all companies are profitable. Early-stage technology companies, biotechnology firms and rapidly expanding businesses often generate meaningful revenue long before they generate sustainable earnings. In such situations, analysts sometimes use the Price-to-Sales (P/S) ratio instead.

The absence of earnings does not eliminate the need for predictability. It merely shifts the focus from earnings to revenue. The same principles therefore continue to apply. Revenue should be visible, relatively stable and exhibit a clear long-term trend. Otherwise, sales alone provide little indication of value.

Asset-Based Valuation

Asset-based valuation is commonly used when a company's earnings are unpredictable or do not adequately reflect its underlying value. Instead of focusing on what the company earns, the emphasis shifts to what the company owns.

Characteristics

This approach works best for companies with the following characteristics:

Asset-Heavy. One reason to use asset-based valuation is that the company owns a substantial amount of assets that form the foundation of its value. In such businesses, the assets themselves often determine the company's worth more directly than the earnings they currently generate. It is therefore more meaningful to value the underlying assets than the earnings arising from those assets.

Reliable Benchmarks. Asset-based valuation relies heavily on objective benchmarks. These benchmarks should be readily available, regularly updated and supported by liquid markets or independent valuations. Examples include quoted share prices for investment portfolios, market prices of comparable properties or book values that have been reviewed by reputable auditors or professional valuers.

Stability. Asset values generally fluctuate less than corporate earnings. As a result, companies with cyclical, volatile or lumpy earnings often produce more stable valuations when valued based on their assets rather than their profits.

Companies commonly valued using this approach include property companies, banks, financial institutions and investment holding companies. It is also frequently applied to companies with cyclical or project-based earnings, such as construction companies, shipbuilders and commodity producers.

Note: One common mistake is to value commodity producers, traders and processors using the same methodology because they all operate within the same industry. In reality, their business models are very different. Commodity producers are exposed directly to fluctuations in commodity prices. Their selling prices rise and fall with the market, while many of their production costs remain relatively fixed. This causes earnings to be highly cyclical, making asset-based valuation more appropriate in many cases.

Commodity traders and processors, however, operate differently. Although their selling prices also fluctuate with commodity prices, their input costs generally move in tandem. Their profit margins are therefore often more stable because increases or decreases in selling prices are largely offset by corresponding changes in raw material costs. As a result, their earnings tend to be more predictable, making earnings-based valuation a more suitable approach.

Once again, this illustrates an important principle. Companies within the same industry do not necessarily share the same business model or valuation methodology. Understanding how a company creates value is essential before deciding how it should be valued.

Methodologies

P/B Ratio. The most widely used asset-based valuation method is the Price-to-Book (P/B) ratio. It compares a company's share price with the book value of its shareholders' equity. Although the P/E ratio is more widely used, the P/B ratio has a broader application because companies that are temporarily loss-making may still possess substantial net assets. As long as shareholders' equity remains positive, the P/B ratio remains meaningful. For this reason, equity strategists frequently use P/B ratios when comparing valuations across different sectors and stock markets.

Like the P/E ratio, the P/B multiple reflects both risk and return. Companies with stronger profitability, lower perceived risks and better growth prospects generally command higher P/B multiples. However, book value is not always an accurate reflection of economic value. Assets may have appreciated significantly over time, particularly land and investment properties acquired many years ago. Conversely, valuable intangible assets such as brands, patents, customer relationships or proprietary technology are often understated or omitted altogether from the balance sheet. Companies generating superior returns on assets (ROA) also tend to deserve higher valuations than companies owning similar assets but generating weaker returns. As a result, P/B ratios cannot be compared blindly across companies or industries without considering the quality of the underlying assets.

RNAV. Another commonly used asset-based valuation methodology is the Realisable Net Asset Value (RNAV). Instead of using the book value of shareholders' equity, RNAV estimates the market value of a company's assets after deducting its liabilities. Companies are then valued based on a discount or premium to their RNAV.

RNAV is particularly common for property developers because many of their land banks were acquired years, or even decades, ago and continue to be carried at historical cost. As a result, the book value of equity often understates the company's true asset value. RNAV adjusts these assets to their estimated market values, providing a more realistic measure of what the business is worth.

Property investment companies, however, can be valued differently. Under prevailing accounting standards, investment properties are commonly revalued on a regular basis, typically with annual assessments by management and periodic independent valuations by professional valuers. Because the carrying values are already updated to reflect market conditions, the book value of equity becomes a much more reliable measure of asset value. Consequently, the P/B ratio is often sufficient for valuing these companies, making RNAV adjustments less necessary.

Cash Flow-Based Valuation

Cash flow-based valuation is generally applied when earnings are not a reliable measure of value. Accounting earnings can be distorted by significant non-cash items such as depreciation, amortisation, impairments or fair value adjustments. In such cases, analysts may focus on cash flows instead, as they better reflect the actual cash generated by the business.

Characteristics

Like earnings-based valuation, cash flow-based valuation requires a high degree of predictability. Cash flows should exhibit the same characteristics of visibility, stability and trend. In fact, the requirements are often even more demanding. This is because methodologies such as the Discounted Cash Flow (DCF) model and the Dividend Discount Model (DDM) project cash flows or dividends many years into the future, often extending to perpetuity. The further the forecast extends, the more sensitive the valuation becomes to small changes in the underlying assumptions.

Cash flow-based valuation is therefore most suitable for businesses with highly predictable long-term cash flows. Typical examples include real estate investment trusts, infrastructure operators, utility companies and businesses operating under long-term concessions or contracts. Although these companies often report lower accounting earnings due to substantial depreciation charges, their operating cash flows remain relatively stable and predictable.

Methodologies

DCF. The DCF model is often regarded as one of the most comprehensive valuation methodologies, because it values a company based on the present value of its entire stream of future cash flows. Personally, I see it more as an academic model for teaching the concepts of valuation, rather than as a practical day-to-day tool for equity research. Its greatest strength is also its greatest weakness. In theory, the DCF captures almost every factor that influences valuation. In practice, the valuation depends on a large number of assumptions, many of which are themselves estimates.

The first major assumption is the discount rate, usually represented by the Weighted Average Cost of Capital (WACC). Calculating the WACC requires estimating both the cost of debt and the cost of equity. The latter is commonly derived using the Capital Asset Pricing Model (CAPM), which itself depends on assumptions such as the beta, the market risk premium and the risk-free rate. Each of these variables can vary depending on the data source, time period and methodology used. Small differences in these assumptions can produce materially different valuations, even when the underlying business remains exactly the same.

The second major assumption is the Terminal Value, which usually represents the largest component of a DCF valuation. Terminal Value is commonly calculated using the Gordon Growth Model, which assumes the company will continue growing at a constant rate into perpetuity. This raises a practical question: If forecasting earnings two or three years ahead is already difficult, how can anyone forecast a company's growth into perpetuity with confidence?

The challenge becomes even greater for high-growth companies. Consider Nvidia, which recorded an EPS growth of 66% for FY2026. How many years can such exceptional growth be sustained? Will growth remain elevated for another three, five or ten years? More importantly, when will it eventually slow towards a perpetual growth rate of 2% or 3%? There is no objective answer. Different analysts will inevitably arrive at different conclusions, leading to very different valuations despite using the same DCF methodology.

The final issue is the length of the explicit forecast period. A shorter forecast period places greater reliance on the Terminal Value, while a longer forecast period requires analysts to make increasingly uncertain long-term assumptions. In a typical three-year DCF forecast, the Terminal Value usually accounts for between 75% and 90% of the total valuation, depending on the assumptions used. Ironically, the largest component of the valuation is derived from the most uncertain assumptions.

As discussed in Chapter 3, we talked about "Garbage In, Garbage Out." A financial model is only as reliable as the assumptions behind it. The same applies to a valuation model. A sophisticated DCF model cannot compensate for unrealistic assumptions. If the inputs are weak, the valuation will be equally unreliable.

Despite these limitations, the DCF remains one of the most widely used valuation methodologies in equity research. In some cases, it is the most appropriate approach, particularly for businesses with highly predictable long-term cash flows. In other situations, however, the DCF can produce valuations that are easier to support than those derived using more conventional methodologies such as the P/E ratio.

For example, a high-growth company may be trading at well over 100 times earnings. Maintaining a Buy recommendation and a high target price using a conventional P/E approach can be challenging because the valuation already appears expensive. A DCF, on the other hand, allows analysts to extend the forecast horizon and assume that the company's exceptional growth continues for many more years before eventually converging towards a perpetual growth rate. These additional assumptions can have a significant impact on the valuation and may produce a much higher target price than conventional valuation methodologies.

Personally, I prefer a much simpler approach. Rather than forecasting cash flows decades into the future, I compare today's share price against the company's forecast earnings over the next three to five years. Once the implied P/E multiple falls to a level that appears reasonable, it provides a good indication of how much future growth has already been priced into the stock. The approach is straightforward, transparent and relies on far fewer assumptions than a DCF. Simpler models may not appear as sophisticated, but fewer assumptions often lead to more reliable conclusions.

DDM and Dividend Yield. The DDM is conceptually similar to the DCF but much simpler. Instead of valuing the company's future cash flows, it values the future stream of dividends expected to be received by shareholders. The model assumes that the company pays a stable dividend that grows at a constant rate into perpetuity. The DDM is therefore most suitable for companies with predictable and sustainable dividend policies. It is commonly applied to mature businesses with stable cash flows and a long history of paying dividends.

Despite its simplicity relative to the DCF, the DDM suffers from many of the same practical limitations. It still requires assumptions about the discount rate, the long-term growth rate and perpetual growth. Small changes in these assumptions can produce significantly different valuations.

In practice, I prefer using dividend yield as a valuation benchmark. Dividend yield allows investors to compare a company's expected dividend return directly with comparable companies and with its own historical trading range. It is therefore a simpler and more transparent approach, while still allowing investors to incorporate their own views on the company's growth prospects and risk profile.

Conceptually, dividend yield plays the same role as a valuation multiple in other valuation methodologies. Just as investors are willing to pay a higher P/E multiple for companies with stronger growth and lower risk, they are generally willing to accept a lower dividend yield for dividend-paying companies with better growth prospects or lower perceived risks.

For example, a REIT with strong rental reversions, a healthy acquisition pipeline and consistent dividend growth may trade at a lower dividend yield because investors are willing to pay a premium for its future prospects. Likewise, a REIT with exceptionally stable income may also command a lower yield because investors perceive its cash flows to be less risky. Conversely, companies with slower growth or greater uncertainty generally need to offer higher dividend yields to attract investors.

EV/EBITDA Ratio. Some investors prefer to value companies based on cash flows rather than accounting earnings. Their concern is that reported earnings can be distorted by financing decisions, accounting policies and large non-cash items such as depreciation, amortisation, impairments or fair value adjustments. By focusing on EBITDA, they attempt to remove much of this accounting noise and evaluate the company's underlying operating performance.

The Enterprise Value-to-EBITDA (EV/EBITDA) ratio is a common cash flow-based valuation methodology. In essence, the EV/EBITDA ratio is very similar to the P/E ratio. While the P/E ratio compares a company's market capitalisation with its net profit attributable to shareholders, the EV/EBITDA ratio compares the Enterprise Value (EV) – comprising market capitalisation plus net borrowings – with EBITDA, which represents earnings before interest, tax, depreciation and amortisation. Because both the numerator and denominator exclude the effects of financing decisions, EV/EBITDA also allows companies with different capital structures to be compared more consistently.

Despite its advantages, EV/EBITDA is not as widely used as the P/E ratio. Calculating EV and EBITDA involves several adjustments and can be cumbersome. Consequently, many investors are less familiar with EV/EBITDA than with the more intuitive P/E ratio. This, in turn, results in a lack of meaningful benchmarks for EV/EBITDA. An experienced analyst can usually tell you whether a company trading at 8 times or 20 times P/E is expensive or cheap, because decades of market experience have created an intuitive feel for earnings multiples. The same intuition is far less common for EV/EBITDA. Most investors simply do not have enough experience with the ratio to judge whether 6 times or 12 times EV/EBITDA represents good value. Without a meaningful benchmark, the ratio becomes little more than a number.

For this reason, although EV/EBITDA has sound theoretical merits and is used extensively in mergers and acquisitions as well as for capital-intensive businesses, it remains less popular with the wider investment community.

Other Valuation Models

The valuation methodologies discussed earlier are the ones most commonly encountered in equity research. However, certain industries possess unique operating characteristics that have given rise to specialised valuation metrics. These metrics are designed to capture the key business drivers of specific industries and are often used alongside the conventional valuation models rather than as substitutes.

Price-to-Order Book. For construction companies, shipyards and engineering contractors, the order book is often the strongest indicator of future earnings. It represents secured contracts that are expected to be recognised as revenue over time. Since reported earnings merely reflect the gradual execution of these contracts, analysts sometimes regard the order book as a more forward-looking measure of the company's earning potential.

The Price-to-Order Book ratio compares a company's market capitalisation with the value of its outstanding order book. A higher multiple generally reflects stronger confidence in the quality, profitability or sustainability of future projects, while a lower multiple may indicate concerns over execution risk, margins or the ability to replenish the order book.

Like EV/EBITDA, however, the ratio suffers from a lack of meaningful benchmarks. Not all companies disclose their order books, and those that do may report them using different definitions. Some report the gross order book (i.e., gross value of secured contracts), while others disclose the net order book (i.e., outstanding balance yet to be recognised as revenue). Differences in contract duration, profit margins and execution risk further reduce comparability. As a result, the Price-to-Order Book ratio is generally used as a supplementary valuation tool rather than a primary valuation methodology.

Sum of the Parts. Some companies, particularly conglomerates, operate several businesses across different industries. As each business has its own business model, earnings characteristics and valuation drivers, it is often inappropriate to value the entire group using a single valuation methodology or valuation multiple. Instead, analysts value each business segment separately using the most appropriate methodology before adding the individual values together. This is known as the Sum-of-the-Parts (SOTP) valuation.

In practice, however, the combined value of a conglomerate is often lower than the sum of its individual parts. This difference is commonly referred to as the **Conglomerate Discount**. The discount arises because diversified groups are generally more complex to understand, analyse and value. Their businesses may operate in unrelated industries with different characteristics. The additional complexity increases uncertainty and therefore reduces the valuation investors are willing to assign.

Another reason is capital allocation. Investors generally prefer companies to focus on businesses where they possess competitive advantages and can achieve greater scale and operating efficiencies. If investors wish to diversify across industries, they can easily do so by constructing their own portfolios. There is therefore little incentive to pay a premium for diversification that they can achieve themselves.

Conglomerates also tend to receive less analyst coverage. Analysing a diversified group requires an analyst to understand several industries, build multiple financial models and apply different valuation methodologies. The time required to cover one conglomerate may be sufficient to cover several specialised companies. As a result, analysts generally focus only on the larger conglomerates with sufficient market capitalisation and trading volume to justify the additional research effort.

Valuation Benchmarks

Selecting the appropriate valuation methodology is only half the exercise. Once the methodology has been chosen, the next question is what valuation multiple should be applied. A P/E valuation, for example, still requires the analyst to decide whether the company deserves 10 times, 15 times or 25 times earnings. Valuation benchmarks help answer this question. Rather than selecting a multiple arbitrarily, analysts compare the company against an appropriate benchmark to estimate a reasonable valuation range. The two most common approaches are peer comparison and historical comparison.

Peer Comparison

Peer comparison is a comparison across space. It compares the target company against other companies with similar characteristics. Ideally, the most suitable peers are companies operating in the same industry and listed on the same stock exchange. Companies within the same industry generally face similar operating environments, customers, competitors and regulatory conditions. They are therefore expected to exhibit comparable business models, financial characteristics and valuation multiples.

Listing on the same stock exchange is equally important because companies are exposed to the same investor base, market liquidity and investment preferences. These factors can have a significant influence on valuation. The importance of market differences can be seen in Chinese companies listed in both mainland China and Hong Kong. Although the underlying businesses are identical, A-shares have often traded at materially different valuations from their H-share counterparts because the two markets have different investors, liquidity profiles and regulatory environments.

In practice, however, ideal peers are not always available. This is particularly true for niche industries or smaller exchanges such as Singapore. Analysts may therefore broaden their comparison to companies listed on other exchanges or businesses with similar operating or valuation characteristics. For example, a high-dividend company may be compared with REITs because both compete for income-focused investors. Nevertheless, every departure from the ideal peer group reduces the reliability of the comparison.

Even the best peer comparison has its limitations. No two companies are identical. Differences in management quality, competitive advantages, operating efficiency, financial strength and corporate governance all influence valuation. Peer comparison should therefore be viewed as a benchmark rather than definitive proof that a company is overvalued or undervalued.

Historical Comparison

Historical comparison is a comparison across time. Instead of comparing a company with others, analysts compare the company against itself. As a company's business grows and evolves through different economic and industry cycles, its valuation multiple changes to reflect changing earnings prospects and investor expectations. By examining how the market valued the company under similar business conditions in the past, analysts can estimate an appropriate valuation multiple today.

Returning to our earlier example of ST Engineering, the historical relationship between its trailing P/E ratio and expected earnings growth provides a useful valuation benchmark. If the company's current growth outlook resembles a previous period, the valuation multiple observed during that period may provide a reasonable reference point.

Historical comparison is particularly useful when suitable peer companies do not exist or when specialised valuation metrics such as EV/EBITDA or Price-to-Order Book lack widely accepted benchmarks. While it may be difficult to judge whether a company trading at 6 times EV/EBITDA is expensive or cheap in absolute terms, it becomes much easier if the company has historically traded in the range of 5 to 10 times. Analysts can then assess whether the current operating outlook justifies a valuation near the top or bottom of that historical range.

Like peer comparison, historical comparison also has limitations. Companies evolve over time. Changes in strategy, acquisitions, business mix and competitive positioning may fundamentally alter the company's valuation characteristics. A manufacturer that successfully transforms into a property developer, for example, should not necessarily be expected to trade at the same valuation multiple it commanded in the past.

Similarly, industries evolve. The emergence of smartphones fundamentally changed the outlook for traditional mobile phone manufacturers and digital camera companies. In such cases, one should not simply apply the historical valuation multiples observed during earlier business cycles. Those multiples reflected temporary cyclical fluctuations within a fundamentally healthy industry. Once the industry undergoes a structural shift, the appropriate valuation benchmark must also change to reflect the weaker long-term earnings prospects. Historical comparisons must therefore always be interpreted within the appropriate business context.

Applying Benchmarks

For an IR consultant, valuation benchmarks are valuable not merely because they help estimate fair value, but because they help explain why a company trades differently from its peers. The differences often reveal opportunities for improvement. If comparable companies command higher valuation multiples because they provide better disclosures or clearer earnings guidance, the company may be able to narrow the valuation gap through improved investor communication. If investors assign higher valuations to peers with stronger dividend policies or more efficient capital structures, these become issues that management and the board may wish to consider.

Nevertheless, not every valuation gap can be closed quickly. Competitive advantages such as stronger brands, proprietary technology or market leadership may take many years to develop. Ultimately, the greatest value of benchmarking lies not in determining whether a company deserves 12 or 15 times earnings. It lies in identifying why the market assigns different valuations to similar companies. Once those reasons are understood, the company can formulate strategies to strengthen its business, improve its communication and, over time, narrow the valuation gap.

Chapter 5

The Pitch

By this stage, the analytical work is complete. You have understood how the company generates its earnings through the business model, forecasted its future performance using the financial model, and estimated its value through the valuation model. The final step is to bring these pieces together into a coherent investment proposition – one that is supported by evidence and resonates with the right investors.

The Target Audience

Not every investment appeals to every investor. Although all investors seek to generate returns, they differ greatly in how they intend to achieve them. Some pursue rapid capital appreciation through high-growth companies. Others prefer the stability of defensive businesses or the recurring income offered by dividend stocks. Some actively seek cyclical opportunities, while others avoid them altogether.

Positioning is therefore about matching a company's strengths with the preferences of the investors who are most likely to appreciate them. Rather than trying to appeal to everyone, an effective IR programme focuses on the audience whose investment objectives best align with the company's underlying characteristics.

Importantly, positioning is not something that needs to be explicitly stated. Investors form their own conclusions based on the information presented to them. Growth investors naturally focus on indicators such as expanding addressable markets, strong competitive advantages and long growth runways. Dividend investors pay closer attention to cash generation, dividend sustainability and balance sheet strength. Defensive investors look for resilient demand and stable earnings through economic cycles. The role of IR is therefore not to tell investors how they should classify the company, but to provide the evidence that allows the right investors to reach that conclusion themselves.

Consistency is equally important. Every communication – from presentations and results announcements to annual reports and the corporate website – should reinforce the same investment proposition. Mixed messages weaken credibility. For example, a company positioned as a growth stock would normally be expected to reinvest aggressively for future expansion rather than distribute most of its earnings as dividends. Conversely, a company positioned as a dividend stock should demonstrate capital discipline and sustainable cash generation rather than pursue aggressive expansion that could compromise future distributions.

Companies often possess characteristics that support more than one investment proposition. A business may reasonably be viewed as a growth stock, a defensive stock or a dividend stock, depending on which aspects of the business are emphasised. The role of the IR consultant is to identify the positioning that best reflects the company's strengths and resonates most strongly with investors under the prevailing market conditions. The following case study illustrates how this analytical process was applied.

CASE STUDY: SHENG SIONG GROUP

In 2011, Financial PR was appointed to advise Sheng Siong Group on its initial public offering (IPO). The first step was to identify the company's possible investment propositions before determining which would be most compelling under the prevailing market conditions.

The Possible Positioning

From our assessment, the possible positioning angles for Sheng Siong include:

Growth Stock. Sheng Siong had a strong expansion track record, continued opening new stores and was steadily increasing its market share. The business generated healthy earnings growth and still had room for further expansion across Singapore.

Defensive stock. Supermarkets sell essential daily necessities. Regardless of whether the economy is booming or in recession, consumers still need to buy groceries. This makes demand relatively stable compared with many other retail businesses. The company also had a disciplined operating model, strong cash generation and resilient earnings.

Dividend stock. The business generated strong operating cash flow, required relatively modest capital expenditure and, importantly, enjoyed a negative working capital cycle. Customers paid immediately when they made their purchases, while suppliers were paid later. As a result, the company consistently accumulated cash despite continuing to expand its operations.

At this stage, there was no right or wrong answer. Each positioning had its own merits and supporting evidence. The next step was to determine which investment proposition offered the strongest appeal under the prevailing market conditions.

The Final Selection

The timing of the IPO was particularly challenging. In 2011, global financial markets were unsettled by the European sovereign debt crisis. Investor confidence was weak, risk appetite had declined and many investors were looking for stability rather than aggressive growth. Companies offering predictable earnings and sustainable dividend income were attracting greater attention than higher-risk growth stories. Against this backdrop, the defensive and dividend stock positioning became much more appealing.

Based on this analysis, we recommended increasing the company's dividend payout ratio from the proposed 50% to 100%. After discussions with management and the IPO advisers, the company eventually adopted a payout ratio of 90%, which implied a dividend yield of 6.6% based on Sheng Siong's FY2010 core earnings and the IPO price of S$0.33.

The market responded positively to Sheng Siong's investment proposition. Despite being launched during a period of heightened market uncertainty, the IPO was 1.3 times oversubscribed, reflecting healthy demand from investors for a defensive, income-generating business. Following its listing, the share price rose to a high of S$0.575 within its first month of trading, representing a gain of around 74% over its IPO price.

This case study illustrates the analytical process introduced throughout this book. We first understood Sheng Siong's business model to identify its strengths. We then assessed how those strengths translated into future earnings, cash flows and valuation. Finally, we considered the prevailing market environment to determine which investment proposition would resonate most strongly with investors.

The positioning was therefore not created through marketing. It emerged from analysis. More importantly, effective positioning is not about telling the most exciting story. It is about identifying the story that is both true to the business and most relevant to investors at that point in time.

The Storyline

While positioning attracts the right investors, it alone rarely causes investors to buy the stock. A company may possess all the characteristics of an attractive investment, yet its share price may remain unchanged because those strengths are already recognised by the market. In an efficient market, known information is already reflected in the share price. Investors therefore need a reason to believe that something is about to improve beyond current expectations. This is where catalysts become important.

The Prospect of Change Is a Call to Action

As discussed in Chapter 1, a catalyst is a development that changes investors' expectations about the company's future earnings or valuation. It provides the trigger for investors to act. Without a catalyst, an undervalued stock can remain undervalued for a long time. With one, the market begins to reassess what the company is worth. Every effective investment story is therefore built around change. It is not enough to explain what the company does well today. The storyline must explain what is changing, why it matters and how that change affects future earnings and valuation.

The storyline almost always revolves around one or more of the company's key business drivers. Suppose a growth company launches a promising new product. Simply describing the product is unlikely to excite investors if the information is already public. The product's existence has already been factored into the share price. The catalyst lies in new information that changes the market's expectations. This could be a major customer order that validates commercial demand, a technological breakthrough that strengthens its competitive advantage, or a new application that significantly expands its addressable market. Each of these developments alters future earnings expectations and therefore changes the company's valuation.

Once the catalyst has been identified, the earlier analytical framework becomes invaluable. The business model explains why the catalyst matters. The financial model estimates how it affects future earnings under different scenarios. The valuation model translates those revised earnings into a new estimate of fair value. In this way, the storyline becomes evidence-based rather than promotional.

Many new IR consultants find this process intimidating. They often ask where new stories can be found when the company has already announced everything that is required under the listing rules. In reality, meaningful catalysts can be found in many areas:

Result announcements. For most listed companies, earnings announcements are the single most frequent source of new catalysts. At first glance, the market appears to react simply because earnings exceeded or fell short of expectations. In reality, investors are reacting to something much deeper. The results often reveal changes in the underlying business drivers that analysts use in their financial models. New trends emerge, assumptions are revised, and expectations for future earnings change.

A good example was Amazon's first-quarter 2015 results. For the first time, Amazon reported the financial performance of Amazon Web Services (AWS) as a separate reporting segment. Investors discovered that AWS had already become a US$1.57 billion quarterly business with exceptionally high operating margins. Until then, many analysts had assumed that the cloud business was merely breaking even. The disclosure fundamentally changed the market's understanding of Amazon's earnings profile, and the share price surged by around 15% to 18% in after-hours trading.

The results announcement triggered the initial re-rating. However, the real opportunity came afterwards. Once analysts understood the economics of AWS, they could build financial models to estimate its long-term growth potential under different scenarios. As investors increasingly recognised AWS as Amazon's primary profit engine, the company entered a prolonged re-rating cycle based on the new storyline. In the six years between April 2015 and November 2021, Amazon's share price increased by more than 800%. The catalyst was not simply stronger quarterly earnings. It was a fundamental change in how investors understood the business model.

Management plans. Some of the most powerful catalysts originate from management itself. Major expansion plans, acquisitions, capacity increases, new technologies, product launches or strategic shifts often reshape a company's long-term earnings outlook. These initiatives can affect revenue growth, operating margins, capital expenditure, gearing and cash flow for many years.

When such plans are announced, their full financial impact is often unclear. This creates an opportunity for IR to develop a compelling investment storyline. By understanding the business model, analysts can identify the key drivers affected by the initiative. The financial model can then quantify different scenarios, while the valuation model estimates the potential impact on fair value. Rather than simply announcing management's plans, IR can help investors understand why those plans matter financially.

Undervalued stocks. Perhaps the most common storyline in IR is also the simplest. Many companies are not fundamentally undervalued because of poor operating performance. Instead, they are undervalued because investors misunderstand the business, overlook important developments or simply pay little attention to the stock. In these situations, the objective is not to invent a new story. It is to explain the existing story more effectively.

The challenge then becomes identifying the reasons behind the valuation discount and developing solutions to address them. Some can be addressed through better communication, while others require improved disclosures, stronger investor engagement or clearer positioning. The objective is not merely to argue that the stock is cheap, but to explain why the market has undervalued the company and what may lead investors to recognise its true value.

CASE STUDY: SASSEUR REIT

Sasseur REIT is the real estate investment trust of the Sasseur Group, a leading owner and operator of outlet malls in China. It was listed on the SGX Mainboard in March 2018 at an IPO price of S$0.80, implying a market capitalisation of S$944 million. At listing, the REIT owned four outlet malls in China, with an appraised portfolio value of around S$1.5 billion. All four properties were leased to the Sasseur Group under long-term master leases. Financial PR acted as IR adviser during the IPO and continued to advise the REIT after listing.

The Problem

By December 2018, barely nine months after listing, Sasseur REIT's share price had fallen from S$0.80 to S$0.64 – a decline of about 20%. The decline was puzzling. Operationally, the REIT had exceeded the financial forecasts presented during its IPO. The business itself was performing well, yet the share price continued to weaken. Rather than assuming the market was wrong, our first step was to understand why investors remained unconvinced. Feedback gathered from analysts, fund managers and investors pointed to four major concerns:

China's Economic Outlook. The first concern was macroeconomic. The US-China trade war had begun in 2018 following the introduction of tariffs by the Trump administration. Negative news surrounding China's economy caused many China-related companies listed in Singapore to underperform. However, this explanation was incomplete. CapitaRetail China Trust (now CapitaLand China Trust), an appropriate benchmark for Sasseur REIT, declined about 12% over the same period – substantially less than Sasseur REIT's 20% decline. This suggested that macroeconomic concerns alone could not explain the entire valuation gap.

The S-chip Discount. The second issue related to investor perception. Singapore investors have historically been cautious towards S-chips because of numerous accounting scandals and corporate governance failures involving China-listed companies. Although Sasseur REIT was managed in Singapore, many investors continued to associate it with Chinese corporate governance risks because of its Chinese sponsor. This concern intensified after news emerged that a contractor had commenced legal proceedings against the REIT relating to construction payments. Operationally, the lawsuit had virtually no impact on the REIT. The malls continued operating normally, and the sponsor had contractually agreed to indemnify the REIT against additional construction liabilities under the sale and purchase agreement. Nevertheless, investor confidence weakened. Sometimes perception matters as much as reality.

Unappreciated Business Model. The third issue proved to be the most interesting. The IPO marketing campaign positioned Sasseur REIT as Asia's first outlet mall REIT and emphasised the rapid growth of China's outlet retail industry. Although these statements were factually correct, they failed to resonate with Singapore investors. Outlet malls are uncommon in Singapore. Most local investors had only visited IMM, which resembles an ordinary suburban shopping mall. Consequently, investors struggled to understand why outlet malls were such a unique and rapidly growing retail format in China. At the same time, Singapore's media frequently highlighted Alibaba's e-commerce dominance and the decline of traditional retail. Instead of reinforcing the investment case, discussions about China's outlet mall industry often created additional scepticism. The issue was therefore not business performance. It was communication.

Limited Earnings Visibility. Finally, investors lacked confidence in the sustainability of future distributions. The IPO prospectus provided only a two-year DPU forecast. Furthermore, the forecast assumed a 100% dividend payout ratio, rental guarantees that would eventually expire, and a fixed Renminbi exchange rate despite an ongoing depreciation against the Singapore dollar. Once these assumptions expired, investors had little basis for forecasting future distributions. The market therefore assigned a lower valuation multiple because future earnings lacked visibility.

Our Solution

Following a strategic review in December 2018, Financial PR and the management of Sasseur REIT established an ambitious objective – to restore the share price to its IPO price within four months despite worsening macroeconomic conditions. Rather than attempting to create new stories, our strategy was surprisingly simple. Each negative driver identified during the diagnostic stage would be addressed individually:

Reframing the China Story. Instead of allowing investors to associate Sasseur REIT with China's exports and manufacturing economy, the investment story was repositioned around domestic consumption. The corporate presentation replaced the slogan "Asia's First Outlet Mall REIT" with a much simpler message: "A Proxy for China's Middle-Class Consumption." This immediately shifted investors' attention towards rising household incomes instead of trade tensions. Additional emphasis was also placed on the REIT's exposure to inland Tier-2 cities, where its malls are located and whose economic growth had historically exceeded that of many Tier-1 cities while being less exposed to export-related industries.

Building Trust. Changing perceptions required more than simply presenting additional facts. Investors first needed confidence in the people behind the business. We expanded the discussion surrounding founder Mr Vito Xu by including his entrepreneurial journey and management philosophy in the Annual Report. Mr Xu also attended the FY2018 results briefing personally, giving investors an opportunity to interact directly with the founder. Trust became a key part of the investment proposition.

Making the Business Model Understandable. The next objective was to improve understanding of the business itself. Working closely with management, we developed a simplified financial model illustrating how retail sales generated by individual malls eventually translated into distributable income for unitholders. Instead of asking investors to accept management's explanation, they could now see the economics for themselves.

The second challenge was geographical. Most Singapore investors had never visited the malls. To overcome this, the team effectively "brought the malls to investors." The corporate presentation began showing individual mall performance, historical revenue trends, membership growth, tenant mix, operating statistics, and mall-specific developments. Rather than discussing China's outlet industry in abstract terms, presentations focused on tangible shopping experiences and events that investors could easily relate to. Successful malls in Singapore such as VivoCity and United Square were used as familiar reference points.

Finally, instead of arguing against negative sentiment surrounding China's economy, the team reinforced its case by citing public statements from global luxury brands such as LVMH, Tiffany and Hermès regarding the continued strength of Chinese consumer demand. Independent evidence proved more persuasive than self-promotion.

Extending Earnings Visibility. The final objective was to improve investors' ability to forecast future distributions. Using the financial model developed together with management, we constructed multiple forward scenarios to demonstrate the effects of lower dividend payout ratios, further Renminbi depreciation, varying revenue growth assumptions, and different operating outcomes. Instead of presenting a single forecast, investors were shown that distributions remained resilient across a range of realistic assumptions. The focus shifted from predicting one outcome to demonstrating the robustness of the business model.

The Outcome

While not every recommendation proposed by the team was implemented, enough changes were adopted to materially improve market understanding. Within two weeks, the corporate presentation was completely redesigned before we conducted an intensive investor marketing campaign throughout January 2019. Investor response improved noticeably. Attendance at the FY2018 results briefing exceeded expectations, with analysts, fund managers and journalists filling two briefing sessions.

Following another set of results that exceeded expectations, the market reacted very differently from previous quarters. Instead of focusing on macroeconomic concerns, investors increasingly recognised the strength and resilience of the underlying business. The share price recovered to S$0.77 immediately after the results announcement before eventually returning to its IPO price of S$0.80 in April 2019, achieving the objective established during the December strategic review.

This case study illustrates that presenting the same storyline from a different perspective can have a profound impact on share price performance. The key is to focus on what truly matters to investors, rather than promoting the company based on personal opinions or assumptions.

Reaching Out

A compelling investment proposition and a clear target audience significantly improve the chances of a successful pitch. The final step is delivery. While investor briefings, site visits and regular communications remain the primary channels for engaging the market, how you execute these activities can make a significant difference to the outcome.

Taking the Initiative

One observation I have made over the years is that many IR consultants adopt a largely reactive approach. They organise investor briefings around results announcements, prepare press releases and presentations only when required, and respond to enquiries as they arise.

Analysts, by contrast, are generally far more proactive. Many analysts begin each day by pitching their latest research to the sales desk before the market opens. They then call their largest institutional clients to ensure their investment views are heard. They go on roadshows, conduct one-on-one meetings with fund managers, gather market feedback and continuously build relationships with investors. More importantly, they do not limit themselves to writing reports during reporting season. The best analysts actively publish research throughout the year whenever they identify new developments, fresh perspectives or changing market assumptions.

IR consultants should adopt the same mindset. Rather than waiting for the next results announcement, actively look for new developments – both within the company and across the industry – that reinforce your investment proposition. Communicate these through announcements, presentations, corporate publications and investor engagement. Reach out regularly to analysts, fund managers and journalists. Pitch new ideas, seek their views and maintain an ongoing dialogue, especially if you have not heard from them or seen research coverage for some time. Companies do not disappear because their businesses deteriorate. More often, they become forgotten amid the hundreds of listed companies competing for investors' attention.

Our success with Sasseur REIT illustrates the advantage of taking the initiative. Having a good investment story was only the beginning. The story did not sell itself. Armed with a revamped corporate presentation, the team embarked on a two-week market blitz before the results blackout period. We met analysts and fund managers extensively to challenge existing perceptions and communicate the revised investment proposition. The strong turnout at the subsequent results briefing demonstrated the effectiveness of that proactive approach.

Simplicity Sells

One of the biggest misconceptions in IR is the belief that lawyers are the best writers and investment bankers are the most professional communicators. As a result, many companies end up writing press releases like legal documents and designing presentations like investment banking pitch books. Neither works particularly well.

As an IR consultant, your primary role is not to impress people with sophisticated language. Your role is to communicate. Investors should not have to decipher long paragraphs, technical jargon or legal disclaimers just to understand the investment case. You do not need sophisticated English. You need simple English that everyone can understand.

Use short sentences. Use concise bullet points. Use charts, diagrams and photographs to explain concepts visually. Every slide should help your audience understand the company more quickly. If your presentation is crowded with dense text, multiple fonts, coloured boxes and unnecessary decoration, you are distracting your audience rather than helping them. The easier it is to understand your message, the more likely your audience will remember it.

Knowing Your Place

Another common mistake is benchmarking against the largest listed companies. Many IR consultants study the presentations and annual reports of blue-chip companies and assume these represent best practice. They imitate what they see without asking why those companies communicate the way they do.

The reality is very different. Large companies such as CapitaLand or Singtel enjoy a natural following because of their size, liquidity and index weighting. Analysts already cover them. Fund managers already own them. Investors will read their announcements regardless of whether the presentation is outstanding or merely adequate.

Most listed companies do not enjoy that luxury. More than 80% of companies listed in Singapore have a market capitalisation of less than S$1 billion. These small- and mid-cap companies compete fiercely for investors' attention. Even relatively large companies such as Sasseur REIT or Hong Leong Finance are considered small players within their respective sectors.

If you represent one of these companies, you cannot afford to produce average communications. You are competing not only for investors' money, but also for their limited time and attention. You need to be proactive in reaching out to investors, and direct and simple in communicating your investment proposition, particularly if your target audience consists mostly of retail investors. Otherwise, your company risks being overlooked in the crowd of listed companies.

Managing Expectations

Earlier in the book, we discussed the importance of managing expectations to build long-term credibility. The real challenge comes when market expectations become unrealistic due to the runaway success of your IR effort. Suppose a company's share price surges on excessive optimism that management knows cannot be delivered. Should the company enjoy the positive attention and hope reality catches up? Or should it temper expectations, knowing that the share price may fall in the short term?

In my view, the answer is straightforward. It is far better to manage expectations early than to disappoint investors later. Allowing unrealistic expectations to build may create temporary excitement, but the eventual correction is usually far more damaging to the company's credibility.

We encountered a similar situation during Sheng Siong Group's IPO. Within one month of listing, the share price had risen about 74% above its IPO price. While this looked encouraging, we recognised a potential problem. The company's previous year's earnings had included substantial one-off gains from the disposal of non-core assets. The upcoming results would therefore struggle to match the previous reported profit on a year-on-year basis, even though the underlying business remained healthy.

Using our market contacts, we identified several major investors who had accumulated the stock after the IPO and reached out to them directly. We explained the impact of the one-off gains and encouraged them to form realistic expectations for the upcoming results. The share price corrected thereafter, but that was exactly the objective.

When Sheng Siong eventually reported a 35.9% decline in net profit for FY2011, the share price barely moved because the outcome was already reflected in market expectations. In other words, the market reacted not to the headline number, but to whether the result differed from what investors had already anticipated. By managing expectations proactively, Sheng Siong preserved its credibility, retained investor confidence and laid the foundation for a long-term relationship with the investment community.

GROWTH STOCKS

Market Positioning

A company expected to deliver above-average earnings growth over the medium to long term. Investors are willing to pay a premium because they believe future earnings will grow faster than the market.

Business Characteristics

- Large and expanding addressable market
- Innovative products or services
- Growing market share
- Strong competitive advantage
- Pricing power
- High barriers to entry
- Expansion into new products or regions
- Continuous reinvestment for future growth

Financial Characteristics

- Strong revenue growth
- Growing earnings
- Expanding profit margins
- High return on equity (ROE)
- High return on invested capital (ROIC)
- Significant capital expenditure or research and development (R&D)
- Low dividend payout
- Strong operating cash flow

Typical Valuation Models

- Forward P/E
- PEG ratio
- DCF

Common Catalysts

- Better-than-expected earnings
- New product launches
- Capacity expansion
- Market expansion
- Acquisitions
- Industry growth
- Positive regulatory developments

Questions Analysts Will Ask

- Is the growth sustainable?
- What drives future growth?
- How large is the addressable market?
- What gives the company its competitive advantage?
- Can margins continue to improve?

Common Mistakes

- Confusing revenue growth with earnings growth.
- Assuming high growth will continue forever.
- Ignoring valuation.

Examples

NVIDIA, Amazon (in its early years), CATL, Aier Eye Hospital

DEFENSIVE STOCKS

Market Positioning

A company with stable earnings that can perform reasonably well regardless of economic conditions.

Business Characteristics

- Essential products or services
- Strong brands
- Recurring demand
- Long customer relationships
- Regulated industries or businesses
- High customer loyalty
- Low demand volatility

Financial Characteristics

- Stable revenue
- Stable profit margins
- Predictable earnings
- Strong cash flow
- Moderate capital expenditure
- Low earnings volatility

Typical Valuation Models

- P/E
- DCF
- EV/EBITDA

Common Catalysts

- Earnings resilience
- Dividend increases
- Industry consolidation
- Interest rate cuts
- Market uncertainty

Questions Analysts Will Ask

- How stable is demand?
- Can margins be maintained?
- Are customers likely to switch?
- What are the regulatory risks?

Common Mistakes

- Assuming defensive means no growth.
- Ignoring regulatory risks.
- Paying excessive valuations for stability.

Examples

Healthcare providers, utilities, consumer staples, water treatment companies

DIVIDEND STOCKS

Market Positioning

A company that generates stable cash flow and returns a significant portion of its profits to shareholders through dividends.

Business Characteristics

- Mature business
- Stable operations
- Limited expansion requirements
- Strong market position
- Disciplined capital allocation

Financial Characteristics

- Strong operating cash flow
- Healthy free cash flow
- Moderate capital expenditure
- Sustainable payout ratio
- Consistent dividend history

Typical Valuation Models

- Dividend Discount Model (DDM)
- P/E
- DCF

Common Catalysts

- Dividend increases
- Special dividends
- Capital recycling
- Asset disposals
- Lower interest rates

Questions Analysts Will Ask

- Is there a dividend policy?
- What is the payout ratio?
- Will future capital expenditure reduce dividends?

Common Mistakes

- Looking only at dividend yield.
- Ignoring payout sustainability.
- Ignoring balance sheet strength.

Examples

REITs, utilities, mature industrial companies

CYCLICAL STOCKS

Market Positioning

A company whose earnings rise and fall with economic or industry cycles.

Business Characteristics

- Sensitive to economic activity
- Commodity exposure
- Industrial demand
- Property development
- Shipping
- Construction
- Consumer discretionary spending

Financial Characteristics

- Highly volatile revenue
- Large margin fluctuations
- Earnings fluctuate with the economy
- Variable cash flow
- Inventory swings

Typical Valuation Models

- Mid-cycle P/E
- EV/EBITDA
- P/B (for certain industries)

Common Catalysts

- Economic recovery
- Commodity price movements
- Interest rate changes
- Government stimulus
- Infrastructure spending

Questions Analysts Will Ask

- Where are we in the cycle?
- How sensitive are earnings?
- How is management navigating the cycle?
- Is the balance sheet strong enough?

Common Mistakes

- Valuing peak earnings.
- Assuming good times will last forever.
- Ignoring balance sheet risk.

Examples

Shipping, airlines, commodities, property developers

RECOVERY STOCKS

Market Positioning

A company whose earnings have been temporarily depressed but are expected to recover.

Business Characteristics

- Turnaround strategy
- New management
- Cost restructuring
- Industry recovery
- Operational improvements
- New growth initiatives

Financial Characteristics

- Weak historical earnings
- Improving margins
- Improving cash flow
- Strengthening balance sheet
- Declining debt

Typical Valuation Models

- Forward P/E
- EV/EBITDA
- DCF

Common Catalysts

- Earnings turnaround
- New contracts
- Cost savings
- Asset disposals
- Industry recovery
- New management execution

Questions Analysts Will Ask

- What caused the downturn?
- Is the recovery sustainable?
- What evidence supports the turnaround?
- What risks remain?

Common Mistakes

- Believing management promises without evidence.
- Assuming every turnaround succeeds.
- Ignoring structural industry decline.

Examples

Post-restructuring or post-pandemic companies

SPECULATIVE STOCKS

Market Positioning

A company with uncertain earnings but significant upside potential if its business model succeeds.

Business Characteristics

- New technology
- Early-stage business
- Clinical trials
- Exploration assets
- Emerging industries
- Unproven business models

Financial Characteristics

- Limited earnings history
- Negative cash flow
- Frequent capital raising
- High earnings volatility
- Significant execution risk

Typical Valuation Models

- Scenario-based DCF
- Sum-of-the-Parts
- RNAV (resource companies)
- Probability-weighted valuation

Common Catalysts

- Clinical trial results
- Regulatory approvals
- Discovery of resources
- Commercialisation
- Strategic partnerships
- Major contracts

Questions Analysts Will Ask

- What is the probability of success?
- How much funding is required?
- What is the downside risk?
- Which assumptions drive the valuation?

Common Mistakes

- Focusing only on upside.
- Ignoring funding risk.
- Ignoring execution risk.
- Overlooking dilution.

Examples

Biotechnology, exploration companies, early-stage technology companies

About the Author

Ang Soo Kee is the Principal Advisor at Financial PR, a leading IR firm in Singapore. Since joining the firm in 2010, he has advised numerous listed companies on IR, corporate positioning and capital market communications. Prior to IR, he built his career across equity research, corporate finance, private equity and banking, giving him first-hand experience from both the investment and corporate perspectives.

Despite his extensive experience, Soo Kee believes credibility should be earned through facts, sound analysis and practical solutions, rather than an impressive résumé or a list of past achievements. As he often says, ***"You should listen to me not because of where I came from, but because what I say makes sense."***

At Financial PR, Soo Kee focuses on developing the next generation of IR consultants. He advocates an evidence-based approach founded on facts, transparency and clear communication. His press releases and presentations are known for their simple English, concise bullet points and highly visual style. As he often reminds his team, ***"Most of our clients are small-cap companies with a large retail investor base. Unlike large-cap companies, you will have to fight for your audience. If you pitch your company with long, wordy presentations filled with technical jargon and legalese, you will fail."***

The Other Side of the Same Coin brings together the training programmes, methodologies and practical experience he has developed over many years at Financial PR. It was written to provide aspiring IR consultants with a practical guide to the profession and to encourage the standards of analysis, communication and professionalism that he hopes will continue to elevate the IR profession.